The Shadow

by Ritchie Perry

Illustrated by Stephen Player

The Characters

TOM LONG
is thirteen. His shadow keeps going missing and he's sure it's up to no good.

RACHEL HOPE
is thirteen and is Tom's girlfriend. She's worried about the shadow too.

ALAN POTTS

is the same age. He is a friend of Tom and thinks Tom is in trouble.

INSPECTOR HOPE

is a policeman and Rachel's father. Tom comes to him with his problem.

Scene One

Inspector Hope and Tom Long are sitting at the table in Inspector Hope's kitchen. Inspector Hope has a cup of coffee in front of him.

INSP. HOPE: Are you sure you don't want a cup of coffee, Tom? There's plenty in the pot.

TOM: I'm sure, thanks.

INSP. HOPE:	How about a Coke? I think Rachel made a mistake and missed one of the cans in the fridge.
TOM:	No, thanks. I'm not thirsty.
INSP. HOPE:	Suit yourself. Are your mum and dad all right? I've been so busy at work, I can't remember the last time I spoke to them.
TOM:	They're fine.
INSP. HOPE:	But you're not. You have something on your mind.
TOM:	Yes.
INSP. HOPE:	Let me guess, then. You've come to talk to me about Rachel.
TOM:	What do you mean?
INSP. HOPE:	Well, you and my daughter have been seeing a lot of each other these past few weeks. I thought you might have come round to tell me you're engaged.
TOM:	*(Sounding shocked)* We can't do that! We're only thirteen!
INSP. HOPE:	I know, Tom. I know. I was only joking!
TOM:	Oh, I see.

(For a moment Inspector Hope looks at Tom without saying anything. Then he nods his head.)

INSP. HOPE: OK, Tom. It's not your mum and dad, it's not Rachel, and you aren't here just to chat to me. That means you must be in some kind of trouble.

TOM: Yes, I am.

INSP. HOPE: What kind of trouble?

TOM: Bad trouble.

INSP. HOPE: Do you want to tell me about it?

(Tom doesn't answer at first. He is very nervous.)

INSP. HOPE: Come on, Tom. You'll feel better once you get it off your chest. And however bad it is, I promise not to bite your head off.

TOM: I know you won't. That's why I came to see you. The trouble is, it sounds so silly.

INSP. HOPE: Why don't you let me be the judge of that?

TOM: All right, but can you do me a favour?

INSP. HOPE: That depends.

TOM: Can this just be between the two of us?

INSP. HOPE: I can't promise anything until I've heard what you have to say, Tom. I'm a policeman. If you've broken the law, I'll have to do something about it.

TOM: I know that, Mr Hope. All I'm asking is that you listen to everything I have to say before

	you do anything.
INSP. HOPE:	I think I can manage that.
TOM:	Good. *(Taking a deep breath before he carries on.)* I think I've tried to kill somebody.

INSP. HOPE:	You've done what?
TOM:	I think I've tried to kill somebody.

(Inspector Hope shakes his head. He doesn't believe Tom.)

INSP. HOPE:	Listen, Tom. It isn't April Fools' Day today. Killing people isn't something you make jokes about.
TOM:	I'm not joking, and I don't think it's funny at all. I'm frightened.
INSP. HOPE:	Let's get this straight, Tom. Are you telling me that you tried to murder somebody?
TOM:	Yes. I think so.
INSP. HOPE:	You keep saying you 'think' you've tried to kill somebody. What exactly do you mean?

(Before Tom can answer, they hear the sound of the front door being opened. A moment later, Rachel Hope and Alan Potts come into the kitchen.)

RACHEL:	Hello, Dad.
INSP. HOPE:	Hello, Rachel. Hello, Alan. Look, I don't want to be rude but Tom and I are having a little talk. Can you two go somewhere else until we're finished?
RACHEL:	It's all right, Dad.
ALAN:	Yeah. We know just what you're talking about.
TOM:	They're here because I asked them to come.
INSP. HOPE:	In that case, you'd better sit down.

(Rachel and Alan sit down at the table.)

RACHEL: How much has Tom told you, Dad?
INSP. HOPE: He says he thinks he's tried to kill somebody. How much do you two know about this?
ALAN: We know as much as Tom does.
INSP. HOPE: Well, I don't. Can you two keep quiet while I finish talking to Tom? Then I'll hear what you have to say.
RACHEL: OK, Dad.
ALAN: No problem.

INSP. HOPE: All right, Tom. Who is it you think you've tried to kill?

TOM: Tony Lamb.

INSP. HOPE: You mean the little boy who fell into the river yesterday?

TOM: That's right.

INSP. HOPE: I know he was nearly drowned, but that was an accident. He slipped down the bank into the river.

TOM: It wasn't an accident. I tried to kill Tony. And I think I tried to kill Mandy Smith as well.

INSP. HOPE: Are you talking about the little girl who was hurt in the park last week?

TOM: Yes.

INSP. HOPE: That was another accident. Mandy fell out of a tree and broke her leg.

RACHEL: That's what it looked like, Dad, but there was more to it.

ALAN: We think Tom did it.

(Inspector Hope shakes his head again. He still doesn't believe what he's hearing.)

INSP. HOPE: Let's take this one step at a time. All three of you say you think Tom tried to kill Mandy Smith. Are you sure?

TOM: Not really.

INSP. HOPE: But you do know that you tried to murder Tony Lamb.

TOM: I'm fairly sure I did.

INSP. HOPE: OK. Why don't you tell me how you did it?

TOM: I don't know.

(Inspector Hope holds his head in his hands for a second. He looks confused.)

INSP. HOPE: This is crazy. *(Turning to Alan and Rachel.)*

|||What have you two got to say? Do you know how Tom is supposed to have done it?
ALAN: | No.
RACHEL: | I don't have a clue.
INSP. HOPE: | But you do think Tom is an attempted murderer?
ALAN: | Of course we don't.
RACHEL: | Tom would never hurt anybody.
INSP. HOPE: | Am I mad, or is everybody else? None of this makes sense.

TOM:	It gets worse. We think it was my shadow that attacked Mandy and Tony.
INSP. HOPE:	Did I hear you right, Tom? Are you saying you think a shadow tried to murder those children?
ALAN:	That's what we all think.
RACHEL:	If we tell you everything that's happened, perhaps you'll understand.
INSP. HOPE:	That sounds like a very good idea. Just start at the beginning and go all the way through.
TOM:	Well, it began last week.
RACHEL:	The three of us were in the park together.
ALAN:	Yes. It was the last day of the holidays.

Scene Two

Flashback: Alan and Rachel are sitting on a bench in the local park. They are near the children's play area. Tom is standing near the swings with another friend, Paul Smith.

ALAN: Looking forward to going back to school tomorrow?

RACHEL: You must be joking.

ALAN: I thought you'd say that! Mind you, at least the weather is better today.

RACHEL: That only makes things worse. It's rained nearly every day for the last two weeks. Now the holidays are almost over, the sun comes out. The weather forecast says it will be fine all next week.

ALAN: Terrific! Knowing that really makes me feel good.

RACHEL: I can think of something that will make you feel even better.

ALAN: What's that?

RACHEL: The maths homework for Mr Brown.

(Alan bangs his forehead with his fist.)

ALAN: Oh no! I'd forgotten all about it.

RACHEL: I thought you might have done.

ALAN: I'll have to do it this afternoon.

RACHEL: It looks like it. Otherwise you'll be in real trouble.

ALAN: Of course, there is one way round it. I could borrow your maths book and copy the answers.

(Rachel laughs.)

RACHEL: I haven't done it either. Tom and I are doing our homework this evening. We're working over at my place.

ALAN: Can I come too?

RACHEL: You can if you bring some crisps. Tom and I are buying cans of Coke.

ALAN: Sure. What time are you starting?

RACHEL: Early. We want to go over to the youth club when we've finished.

ALAN: Fine. I wouldn't want to miss the disco.

RACHEL: You wouldn't, not when you know Anne Parker is going to be there.

ALAN: What do you mean?

RACHEL: Come off it, Alan. I've seen you. You can't keep your eyes off her.

ALAN: Well, I suppose I do like her a bit.
RACHEL: Anne likes you too.

ALAN:	Does she? How do you know?
RACHEL:	Girl talk. Anne told me.
ALAN:	What did she say?
RACHEL:	She asked me if I knew why you just looked at her and never said a word. I told her you were shy.
ALAN:	You rat. You didn't, did you?
RACHEL:	Yes, I did. It's true.
ALAN:	Maybe it is, but I don't say anything about you to Tom.
RACHEL:	There's nothing to say.
ALAN:	Don't worry. I'll soon think of something. Anyway, when are Tom and Paul coming over to join us? I thought we were all going into town together.
RACHEL:	Paul can't come.
ALAN:	Why's that?
RACHEL:	His mum and dad have gone out. That means he has to look after his little sister, Mandy.
ALAN:	I bet Paul's pleased! What about Tom?
RACHEL:	He should be over in a moment.
ALAN:	Tom must have heard you. He's coming over now.

(Tom leaves Paul and walks towards the bench.)

RACHEL: What's wrong with him?
ALAN: What are you talking about?
RACHEL: I'm not sure, but there's something not right about Tom.
ALAN: So what's new? I've known that for years!
RACHEL: I'm not joking. There's something wrong.
ALAN: Well, I can't see it. Tom looks just as ugly as ever!

(Tom reaches the bench and sits down beside Rachel and Alan.)

TOM: Are you two talking about me?

ALAN: You've guessed. You must have heard me use the word ugly!

TOM: Look who's talking. You've got a face that cracks mirrors!

RACHEL: Shut up, you two. You're acting like babies.

TOM: What's got into you?
ALAN: It's love. She's worried about you.
TOM: What on earth for?
RACHEL: There's something strange about you. Are you sure you're all right, Tom?
TOM: I'm fine. Paul's the one you should be worrying about.
ALAN: Why's that?
TOM: I'll give you three guesses. Look who poor Paul is stuck with.

(Tom points across at Mandy. She has left the swings and is running across the grass towards the small wood at the edge of the park. Paul is walking along behind her.)

RACHEL: We were talking about that before you came over.
ALAN: I was saying how pleased Paul must be!
TOM: Pleased isn't the word. Mandy is a little monster.
RACHEL: Come on, Tom. She can't be that bad.
TOM: No. She's much worse.
ALAN: That's right, Rachel. We see a lot more of Paul than you. You don't know Mandy the way we do.
RACHEL: She's been all right when I've met her.

TOM: In that case, Mandy must have been with her parents.

RACHEL: She was.

ALAN: That explains it. Mandy only shows her true colours when Paul is in charge of her.

TOM: Alan's right. Look at Mandy now. She knows she isn't allowed to go into the woods on her own.

ALAN: You can hear Paul shouting at Mandy from here.

(They all watch Mandy disappear into the woods. Paul starts to run after her. He is shouting for Mandy to come back.)

RACHEL: Perhaps you're right.
ALAN: We are. Anyway, Mandy is Paul's problem. Are we going to sit around here all day?
TOM: Not likely. We can't waste the last day of the holidays.

(Rachel looks at her watch.)

RACHEL: If we hurry, we can catch the 10.30 bus. I have some shopping to do.
TOM: What are you going to buy?
RACHEL: I told you yesterday. If you had listened you'd know I need some new jeans!
ALAN: That sounds exciting.
RACHEL: You don't have to come with me if you don't want to.
TOM: Don't worry. We won't!
ALAN: No, we'll be eating a Big Mac in McDonald's.
TOM: That sounds like a great idea. Let's get going.

(They all stand up.)

RACHEL: I know what it is.
ALAN: What is?
RACHEL: I know what's wrong with Tom.

TOM: There's nothing wrong with me.
RACHEL: Yes, there is. You don't have a shadow.
TOM: Of course I do.
ALAN: No, you don't. Rachel's right.

TOM: There isn't enough sun.

RACHEL: Yes, there is. I have a shadow.

ALAN: So do I. Look.

TOM: Mine must be under me.

(Tom takes two steps, looking down at the ground.)

RACHEL: Your shadow still isn't there. You must have lost it.

ALAN: Perhaps you've turned into a vampire. They don't have shadows.

TOM: Don't be so ...

(Tom stops. They can all hear shouting coming from the wood.)

TOM: That sounds like Paul.

RACHEL: It is. He must be shouting for Mandy.

ALAN: No, he isn't. Paul's shouting for help.

TOM: You're right. Paul must be in trouble.

RACHEL: Well, don't just stand there. Let's go and find out what the problem is.

(Tom, Rachel and Alan run towards the wood. Paul's shouts are getting louder and louder.)

Scene Three

Inspector Hope's kitchen. Inspector Hope, Tom, Rachel and Alan are sitting at the table.

INSP. HOPE: Don't stop. What happened next?

ALAN: We all ran across the park to the wood. That's where we found Paul and his sister.

INSP. HOPE: OK. That's fine, but I need to know exactly what you saw.

RACHEL: It was terrible, Dad. The little girl was lying on the ground and there was a broken branch lying beside her. I could see what had happened at once.

INSP. HOPE:	You could see that Mandy Smith had fallen out of the tree?
RACHEL:	Yes.
INSP. HOPE:	How about Paul? What was he doing?
TOM:	He was crying. He was standing beside Mandy with the tears running down his cheeks. He didn't know what to do.
ALAN:	I don't think he even knew what was happening. He kept on shouting for help even after we came.
INSP. HOPE:	Was there anybody else there?
RACHEL:	No. There weren't many people in the park and nobody else had heard Paul shouting.
INSP. HOPE:	So it was down to you three to help him.
RACHEL:	Yes.
INSP. HOPE:	Tell me what you did.
TOM:	Rachel went to have a look at Mandy. Alan and I tried to calm Paul down.
ALAN:	He was in a terrible state. He kept crying and saying it was all his fault.
TOM:	Yeah. Paul was saying that if he'd stayed with Mandy, she wouldn't have fallen out of the tree. He wouldn't listen when we told him it was an accident.

INSP. HOPE:	What about you, Rachel? Did you move the little girl?
RACHEL:	No. I didn't touch her. I could see that Mandy had been knocked out and her leg was all twisted. I thought she must have broken it.
ALAN:	That's what Rachel told us. We knew we had to go and fetch help.
RACHEL:	Tom runs the fastest so we sent him.
INSP. HOPE:	Where did you go, Tom?
TOM:	There are some houses just the other side of the wood. I ran there. There was a woman in one of the back gardens hanging out washing. I told her there had been an accident and asked her to phone for help. Then I ran back to the others.
ALAN:	It seemed like ages before the ambulance came but it can only have been a few minutes.
INSP. HOPE:	You all seem to have done very well.
RACHEL:	I told you about it before, Dad.
INSP. HOPE:	I know you did, but Tom and Alan weren't here then to tell their part.
TOM:	We only did what we had to, Mr Hope.
ALAN:	Anybody would have done the same.
INSP. HOPE:	I'm not so sure about that. Anyway, there's

still one thing I don't understand. Where does Tom's shadow come into it? You all say it was an accident, that Mandy Smith *fell* out of the tree.

RACHEL: I thought I told you. Tom didn't have his shadow when he was in the park.

INSP. HOPE: And that makes Tom an attempted murderer?

ALAN: Not Tom, Mr Hope. It was his shadow. We think it pushed Mandy out of the tree.

INSP. HOPE: Is that what you think, Tom?

(Tom nods his head. He is looking miserable.)

TOM: Yes, I do.

INSP. HOPE:	Why? It doesn't make sense to me. Did Mandy or Paul say anything about seeing a shadow in the wood?
TOM:	We didn't ask them.
INSP. HOPE:	But they didn't say anything about seeing a shadow, did they? They would have done if they'd seen anything.
RACHEL:	You don't understand, Dad. Tom didn't have his shadow in the park but he did when he ran off to get help. I saw it.
ALAN:	So did I.
TOM:	My shadow must have been waiting for me in the wood.
INSP. HOPE:	Stuff and nonsense! I can think of lots of reasons why you didn't have a shadow for a minute or two. There could have been a small cloud overhead, something like that. What I can't think of is any way a shadow could push a child out of a tree. Can any of you?
RACHEL:	No, Dad, but ...
INSP. HOPE:	I don't want any 'buts'. Can you or can't you?

(*Tom, Rachel and Alan look at each other. Then they slowly shake their heads.*)

INSP. HOPE: Exactly. I really don't know why you think Tom's shadow had anything to do with the Smith girl's accident. There doesn't seem to be anything at all suspicious about it. What on earth put such a strange idea into your heads?

TOM: Look, Mr Hope, we didn't have any idea at the time. We thought it was an accident just like everybody else.

ALAN:	That's right. We saw that Tom didn't have a shadow, but we didn't know that the shadow had anything to do with Mandy falling out of the tree.
INSP. HOPE:	But now you do?
RACHEL:	We think we know.
INSP. HOPE:	OK. Tell me what made you change your minds.
TOM:	It was what happened yesterday.
INSP. HOPE:	Do you mean when Tony Lamb fell into the river?
ALAN:	Yes. We were there at the river when it happened. We saw everything.
INSP. HOPE:	So you saw Tom's shadow do it?
RACHEL:	Of course we didn't, Dad. It isn't as easy as that.
INSP. HOPE:	I didn't think it would be. Why don't you explain exactly what you did see?

Scene Four

Flashback: Rachel, Tom and Alan are standing on the bridge, looking down at the river. Mr and Mrs Lamb are sitting on the river bank about a hundred metres away.

TOM: How old is Tony now?

ALAN: I'm not sure. I think he's four.

RACHEL: No, Tony is older than that. He's been at school for almost a year. I think he must be five.

TOM: Whichever it is, he shouldn't be that close to the river. It's dangerous.

ALAN: He's all right. His mum and dad are there with him.

RACHEL: If Tony did fall in, they wouldn't be able to do much to help. The current is really strong here.

TOM: That's just what I was thinking. I wouldn't like to fall in and I'm a strong swimmer.

ALAN: Tony is wasting his time anyway. He could stand there for a year with his fishing rod and he wouldn't catch a thing. I haven't seen a fish all day.

RACHEL: I can't remember the last time I saw a fish in this part of the river.

TOM: Nor can I. There haven't been any since they opened the new factory.

RACHEL: It's the same with the butterflies. There used to be hundreds every year in the bushes along the river bank. Now you never see any.

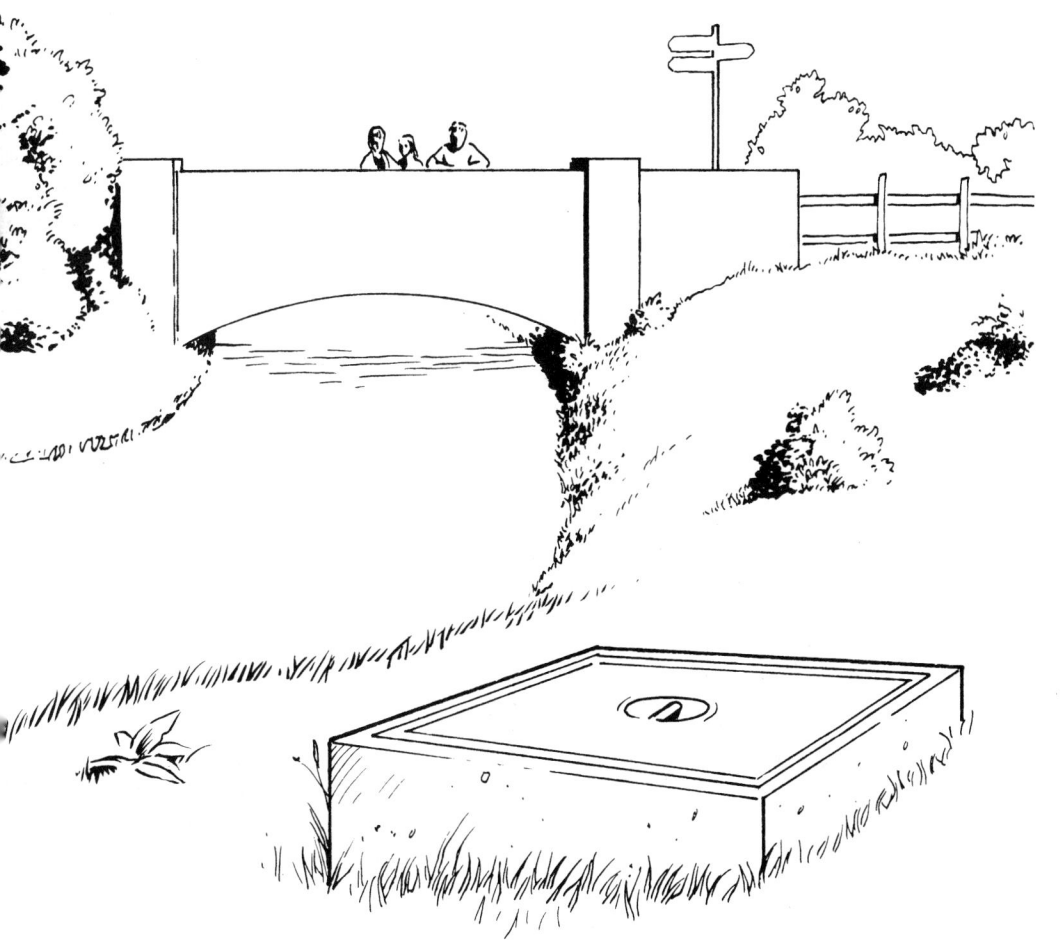

TOM:	That's not because of the factory. It's all the sprays the farmers use on the fields.
ALAN:	I'll tell you something else you don't see any more.
RACHEL:	What's that?
ALAN:	Tom's shadow. Look. It's gone missing again.

(All three look down at the ground. Alan and Rachel have long shadows in the bright sunlight. Tom has no shadow at all.)

TOM:	I don't believe it.
RACHEL:	It's true. You can see for yourself.
ALAN:	Tom really must be a vampire.
RACHEL:	I don't know. He could be the new Peter Pan. He lost his shadow too. In the end, he had to have it sewn back on.
TOM:	It isn't funny. *(Looking all around.)* It must be here somewhere.
ALAN:	If it is, I can't see it.
RACHEL:	Perhaps your shadow was too hot and went for a swim in the river!
TOM:	Ha, ha, ha! That's very amusing, I don't think.
ALAN:	I know. We could go over and ask Mr and Mrs Lamb if they've seen a stray shadow walking past.

(Tom pretends to punch Alan and Alan ducks away. At this moment, they hear a yell. When they look up, they see Tony Lamb in the water.)

RACHEL: Oh no! Tony really has fallen into the river.
TOM: He'll be drowned.
ALAN: Not if we're quick, he won't. Come on.
(They all start to run across the bridge to the river bank.)

Scene Five

Rachel, Tom and Alan are sitting with Inspector Hope in the kitchen of his house.

INSP. HOPE: I gather that you weren't quite quick enough.

RACHEL: No. Tony was swept under the bridge before we could reach the bank. It was Mr Lamb who jumped into the river after him. When he managed to grab hold of Tony, we helped pull both of them up on to the bank.

INSP. HOPE: It sounds as if Tony was lucky not to be drowned.

ALAN: That's right. It's a good job Mrs Lamb is a nurse. There was ever so much water in Tony's lungs. She had to work on him for ages before he could breathe properly.

INSP. HOPE: It must have been quite an experience for all of you. I know how upset Rachel was and it must have been the same for you two boys. There's one thing you seem to have missed out, though. What was Tom's shadow doing?

TOM: We told you. My shadow had gone missing.

RACHEL: Don't you see, Dad? Tom didn't have his shadow and Tony Lamb was nearly killed.

INSP. HOPE: I still don't see what a shadow has to do with what happened. Tony fell into the river. It was an accident.

ALAN: He didn't just fall in. He was pushed.

INSP. HOPE: What do you mean?

TOM: We saw it happen. Tony didn't slip down the bank into the river like the newspaper said.

RACHEL: He suddenly shot forwards into the water. It looked as if somebody or something had given Tony a good shove.

ALAN: That's the way it looked to me too.

INSP. HOPE: OK. Did any of you see Tom's shadow standing behind Tony?

(They shake their heads.)

INSP. HOPE: Of course you didn't, and nor did Mr and Mrs Lamb. Shadows can't push. Shadows can't try to kill people.

RACHEL: How do you know?

ALAN: Yes. How can you be sure?

INSP. HOPE: Well, for one thing, I've never heard of a shadow being blamed for killing somebody before. Have any of you?

Tom:	There's a first time for everything.
Insp. Hope:	Maybe, but just think about it. A shadow is simply a patch of ground that sunlight can't reach because something is in the way. A shadow doesn't have a body. It can't do anything on its own.
Rachel:	That's what people think, Dad. They could be wrong.
Alan:	Tom's shadow could be different. I mean, I've never heard of any other shadow that goes missing.
Insp. Hope:	Nor have I. On the other hand, like I said before, I can think of lots of ways it might have happened.
Tom:	We can too, Mr Hope. We've done nothing else except talk about it since yesterday.
Rachel:	The trouble is, Dad, we always come back to the same thing. Two little children have nearly been killed in the last week and we were there both times.
Alan:	And both times the accidents happened when Tom's shadow went missing.
Insp. Hope:	All right. There's no need to go on because I can see what you're saying. It's a coincidence,

	nothing more.
TOM:	How do you know? How can you be so sure?
RACHEL:	All we know for sure is that Tom's shadow has vanished twice and both times somebody has nearly been killed.
ALAN:	We just can't take the risk of it happening again.
INSP. HOPE:	I still think you're wrong.
TOM:	I hope we are, but it's like Alan said. We can't take the risk.
ALAN:	We don't want anybody else to be hurt. Next time somebody might be killed.

(Inspector Hope holds up his hands.)

INSP. HOPE: OK, OK. You've all had your say and now I need some time to think. Why don't we all have some tea and biscuits? None of you will mind if Mrs Hope joins us, will you?

TOM: I didn't know she was at home.

INSP. HOPE: She's upstairs.

RACHEL: Really? It isn't like Mum to be so quiet.

INSP. HOPE: She must be having a nap. I'll give her a shout.

(Inspector Hope walks over to the kitchen door and opens it. Rachel, Tom and Alan go over to stand behind him.)

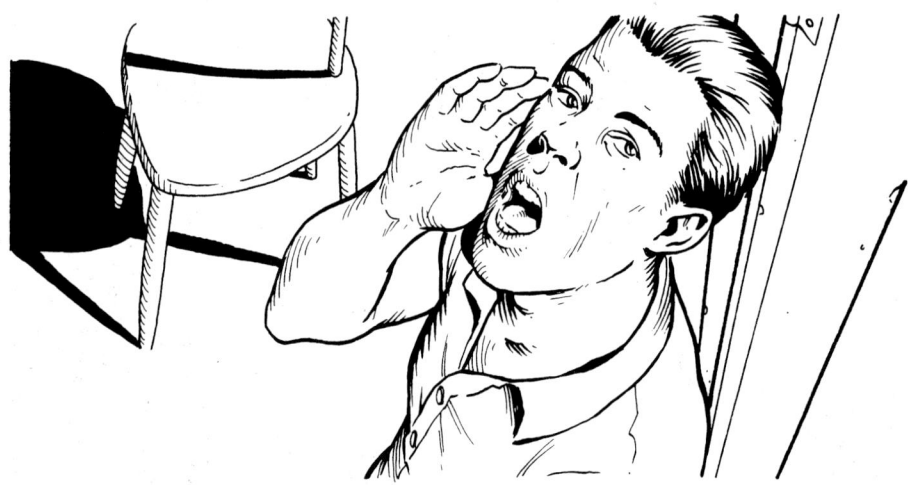

INSP. HOPE: Ellen! *(There is no reply, so he shouts louder.)* Ellen!

(There is still no reply.)

RACHEL: Are you sure Mum is upstairs?

ALAN: If she is, she must be really fast asleep.

TOM: *(Sounding frightened)* It could be a lot worse than that.

INSP. HOPE: What are you talking about?

TOM: Look down at my feet.

RACHEL: Oh no, Tom! Your shadow isn't there.

ALAN: It's happening again.

TOM: My shadow might have gone upstairs. It could be after Mrs Hope.

INSP. HOPE: Good God! *(Shouting)* Ellen! Ellen! Are you all right?

(They all rush towards the stairs with Inspector Hope in the lead.)

THE END